CHICAGO

A MUSICAL VAUDEVILLE

BOOK BY
FRED EBB and BOB FOSSE · MUSIC BY JOHN KANDER · LYRICS BY FRED EBB

BASED ON THE PLAY "CHICAGO" BY MAURINE DALLAS WATKINS

VOCAL SELECTION

chappell music company

MUSICAL CONTENTS

ACT I

ACT II

A MUSICAL VAUDEVILLE

Opening Night June 3, 1975
at the Forty-Sixth Street Theatre, New York

Produced by
ROBERT FRYER and JAMES CRESSON

In Association with
MARTIN RICHARDS
JOSEPH HARRIS and IRA BERNSTEIN

Directed and Choreographed by
BOB FOSSE

Settings by TONY WALTON
Costumes by PATRICIA ZIPPRODT
Lighting by JULES FISHER
Musical Director STANLEY LEBOWSKY
Orchestrations by RALPH BURNS
Dance Music Arranged by PETER HOWARD
Sound Design by ABE JACOB
Hair Styles by ROMAINE GREEN

Production Photos courtesy of The Merlin Group Ltd.

BOB
FOSSE

BOB FOSSE (Director/Choreographer/Co-Author) in 1973 became the first director in history to win the Oscar, Tony and Emmy Awards in a single year for his spectacular triumphs in the film version of CABARET, the Broadway musical PIPPIN, and the television special LIZA WITH A Z. He won the first of his seven Tony Awards as choreographer for PAJAMA GAME, followed by such Broadway credits as the direction and choreography for SWEET CHARITY (as well as the film version), REDHEAD, and LITTLE ME; and the choreography for DAMN YANKEES, NEW GIRL IN TOWN, and HOW TO SUCCEED IN BUSINESS WITHOUT REALLY TRYING. For the screen, he's choreographed MY SISTER EILEEN, PAJAMA GAME, and DAMN YANKEES and this year was nominated for an Academy Award as Best Director for the United Artists film LENNY. His last two performing stints were on stage with the New York City Center dancing the title role in their revival of PAL JOEY and, more recently, on the screen dancing the role of The Serpent in Stanley Donen's musical fantasy, THE LITTLE PRINCE.

JOHN KANDER   FRED EBB

JOHN KANDER (Composer) and FRED EBB (Lyricist/Co-Author) won a Tony, Drama Critics Circle and Grammy Award for their score of the Broadway musical CABARET, while the film version garnered eight Oscars. They first combined talents to create the hit single "My Coloring Book" and then "I Don't Care Much" for Barbra Streisand. Their Broadway collaboration began with FLORA, THE RED MENACE, and has continued through CABARET, THE HAPPY TIME, ZORBA, 70 GIRLS, 70 and now CHICAGO. Most recently, they wrote the Emmy Award winning television special LIZA WITH A Z and Frank Sinatra's return to show business OLE BLUÉ EYES IS BACK. They contributed all the new material for the Barbra Streisand/James Caan movie FUNNY LADY and wrote the background music and title song for the Academy Award winning short subject NORMAN ROCKWELL. One of their happiest assignments was writing and producing CHITA PLUS TWO, a nightclub act for Chita Rivera.

GWEN VERDON

GWEN VERDON (Roxie Hart) has appeared in CAN-CAN, DAMN YANKEES, NEW GIRL IN TOWN, REDHEAD, and SWEET CHARITY. Her awards include 4 Tonys, 2 Donaldsons, a Front Page, Drama Critics Circle, Dance Magazine, Grammy and Mother of the Year Award. She is on the Board of Trustees of the Postgraduate Center for Mental Health, the Board of Directors of the Churchill School, and is very active on the Board of Directors of the New York Public Library, Lincoln Center Branch. Miss Verdon is the mother of Nicole Fosse, age 12.

Photo by KENN DUNCAN

CHITA RIVERA

CHITA RIVERA (Velma Kelly) is happy to be back on the East Coast after spending seven years in California. She has appeared in over 20 straight plays and musicals, most notably creating the role of Anita in both the London and New York productions of WEST SIDE STORY. She duplicated in London her great Broadway success as Rose in BYE BYE BIRDIE and recently created a sensation in New York and Los Angeles with her nightclub act CHITA PLUS TWO produced by Fred Ebb and Ron Field with special material by Kander and Ebb and featuring Tony Stevens and Christopher Chadman. Still and all, the only production she cares to speak about is her favorite—her daughter Lisa.

JERRY ORBACH

JERRY ORBACH (Billy Flynn) last appeared on Broadway in the romantic comedy success 6 RMS RIV VU. He won a Tony Award for his starring role in the musical PROMISES, PROMISES and, earlier, received unanimous raves for his virtuoso performance in SCUBA, DUBA. In 1960, Mr. Orbach created the role of El Gallo in the off-Broadway milestone THE FANTASTICKS, introducing the hit song "Try To Remember," and, the next year, made his Broadway debut opposite Anna Maria Alberghetti in CARNIVAL. He received his first Tony nomination for his portrayal of Sky Masterson in the City Center revival of GUYS AND DOLLS and has played the leading roles off-Broadway in THREEPENNY OPERA and THE CRADLE WILL ROCK. Most recently, he co-starred opposite Maureen Stapleton in THE ROSE TATTOO for the Philadelphia Drama Guild and was seen as Kid Sally in the film THE GANG THAT COULDN'T SHOOT STRAIGHT.

AND ALL THAT JAZZ

Lyrics by FRED EBB

Music by JOHN KANDER

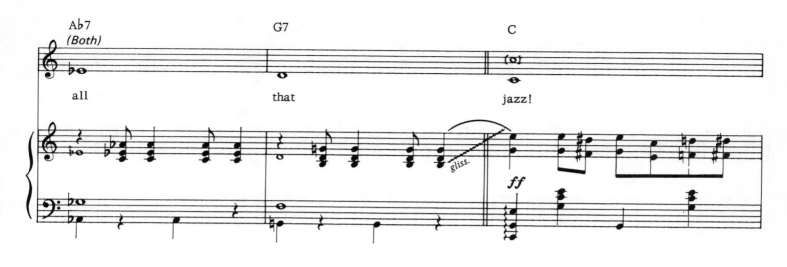

all   that   jazz!

FUNNY HONEY

Lyrics by FRED EBB

Music by JOHN KANDER

That sun - ny, fun - ny, hon - ey hub - by of ___

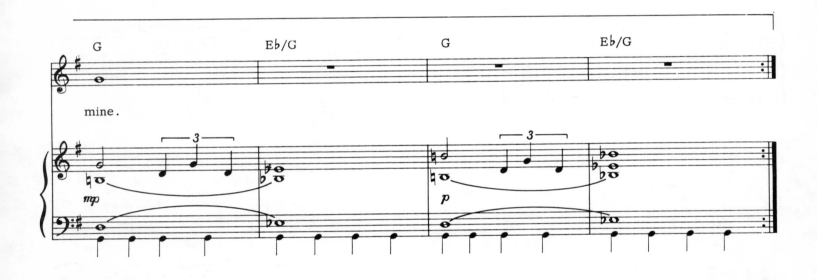

mine.

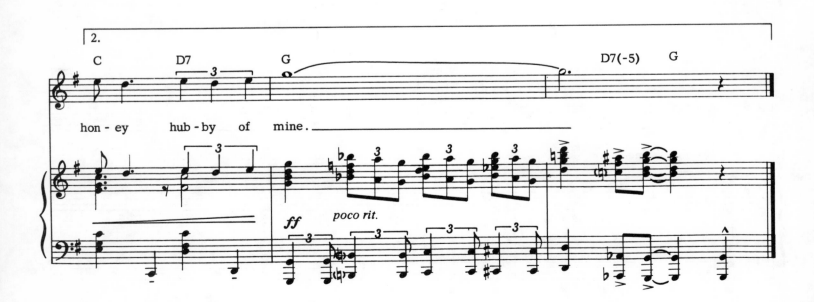

hon - ey hub - by of mine. ___

WHEN YOU'RE GOOD TO MAMA

Lyrics by FRED EBB

Music by JOHN KANDER

All I Care About

Lyrics by FRED EBB

Music by JOHN KANDER

A Little Bit of Good

Lyrics by FRED EBB

Music by JOHN KANDER

ROXIE

Lyrics by FRED EBB

Music by JOHN KANDER

MY OWN BEST FRIEND

Lyrics by FRED EBB

Music by JOHN KANDER

ME AND MY BABY

Lyrics by FRED EBB

Music by JOHN KANDER

1. Me and my ba - by, my ba - by and me, _____ We're 'bout as hap -
2. Look-a my ba - by, my ba - by and me, _____ A dream of a du -
3. Look-a my ba - by, my ba - by and me, _____ Fac - ing the world _____

- py as ba - bies can be. _____ What if I find _____ that I'm
- o, now don't you a - gree? _____ Why keep it mum _____ when there's
- op - ti - mis - ti - cal - ly; _____ Noth - in' can stop _____ us, so

MISTER CELLOPHANE

Lyrics by FRED EBB

Music by JOHN KANDER

If some-one stood up in a crowd and raised his voice up way out loud and
pose you was a lit-tle cat re-sid-in' in a per-son's flat, who

waved his arm and shook his leg, you'd no-tice him.
fed you fish and scratched your ears; you'd no-tice him. If Sup-

some-one in the mov-ie show yelled "Fire____ in the sec-ond row! This
pose you was a wom-an, wed and sleep-in' in a dou-ble bed be-

RAZZLE DAZZLE

Lyrics by FRED EBB

Music by JOHN KANDER

NOWADAYS

Lyrics by FRED EBB

Music by JOHN KANDER

CLASS

Lyrics by FRED EBB

Music by JOHN KANDER